Introduction to Programming with Laravel

In the dynamic world of web development, choosing the right framework can make the difference between a successful project and one that falls short. Laravel has established itself as the most popular and respected PHP framework, and for good reasons. This beginner's manual will guide you through your first steps in Laravel development, from the most basic concepts to building your first functional web application.

Laravel was created by Taylor Otwell in 2011 with a clear mission: to make the web development process enjoyable for the programmer without sacrificing application functionality. Over the years, Laravel has evolved into a complete ecosystem that provides all the necessary tools to build modern and robust web applications.

Why Laravel? The answer is simple: Laravel combines best practices of modern web development with a surprisingly accessible learning curve. The framework incorporates advanced concepts such as dependency injection, MVC (Model-View-Controller) pattern, an elegant ORM (Eloquent), and a powerful templating system (Blade), all while maintaining clear syntax and comprehensive documentation.

This manual is designed with developers taking their first steps in modern PHP and Laravel in mind. We don't assume any prior knowledge beyond a basic understanding of PHP and web development fundamentals. Throughout these pages, we will gradually build your understanding of the framework, starting with fundamental concepts and moving toward more sophisticated features.

What you'll find in this manual:

- A complete introduction to the Laravel ecosystem

- Step-by-step setup of your development environment

- Detailed explanations of key framework concepts

- Practical examples and exercises to reinforce your learning

- Best practices and common design patterns

- Guides to avoid frequent mistakes

Each chapter is structured to build upon knowledge acquired in previous ones, with practical examples that you can follow in your own development environment. Additionally, we include exercises at the end of each section so you can test your understanding and experiment with the code on your own.

By the end of this manual, you will have a solid foundation in Laravel development. You'll be able to create basic web applications, understand the framework's architecture, and most importantly, you'll have the necessary tools to continue your learning independently.

Remember that programming is a continuous learning journey. Don't get discouraged if some concepts seem complex at first; with practice and persistence, each piece of the puzzle will find its place. Laravel has one of the most active and welcoming communities in the web development world, and you'll always find resources and help when you need them.

Let's begin this journey together and discover the power and elegance of Laravel!

Chapter 1: Getting Started with Laravel

What is Laravel?

Laravel is an open-source PHP framework created by Taylor Otwell in 2011. Its main philosophy focuses on providing an elegant and expressive development experience, eliminating much of the complexity traditionally associated with PHP development.

System Requirements

Before starting with Laravel, ensure your system meets the following requirements:

- PHP >= 8.1
- PHP Ctype Extension
- PHP cURL Extension
- PHP DOM Extension
- PHP Fileinfo Extension
- PHP Filter Extension
- PHP Hash Extension
- PHP Mbstring Extension
- PHP OpenSSL Extension
- PHP PCRE Extension
- PHP PDO Extension
- PHP Session Extension
- PHP Tokenizer Extension
- PHP XML Extension

Installation

Installation via Composer

Composer is the standard dependency manager for PHP. To install Laravel, run:

```
composer create-project laravel/laravel my-project
cd my-project
php artisan serve
```

Project Structure

After installation, Laravel creates an organized directory structure:

```
/app           # Main application code
/bootstrap     # Framework bootstrap files
/config        # Configuration files
```

```
/database      # Migrations and seeders
/public        # Entry point and public assets
/resources     # Views, uncompiled assets
/routes        # Route definitions
/storage       # Application-generated files
/tests         # Automated tests
/vendor        # Composer dependencies
```

Initial Configuration

.env File

The .env file contains environment-specific configuration. You should configure:

```
APP_NAME=ApplicationName
APP_ENV=local
APP_KEY=base64:your-generated-key
APP_DEBUG=true
APP_URL=http://localhost

DB_CONNECTION=mysql
DB_HOST=127.0.0.1
DB_PORT=3306
DB_DATABASE=database_name
DB_USERNAME=user
DB_PASSWORD=password
```

Generating Application Key

```
php artisan key:generate
```

Artisan CLI

Artisan is Laravel's included command-line interface. Some useful commands:

```
# List all available commands
php artisan list

# Create a controller
php artisan make:controller UserController

# Create a model
php artisan make:model User

# Create a migration
php artisan make:migration create_users_table
```

Your First Route

In routes/web.php, you can define your first route:

```
Route::get('/', function ()
    { return view('welcome');
});

Route::get('/hello', function () {
```

```
    return 'Hello, Laravel!';
});
```

Your First View

In `resources/views`, **create** `hello.blade.php`:

```
<!DOCTYPE html>
<html>
<head>
    <title>My First View</title>
</head>
<body>
    <h1>Welcome to Laravel</h1>
    <p>This is your first view with Blade</p>
</body>
</html>
```

Your First Controller

```
php artisan make:controller HelloController
```

In `app/Http/Controllers/HelloController.php`:

```php
<?php

namespace App\Http\Controllers;

use Illuminate\Http\Request;

class HelloController extends Controller
{
    public function index()
    {
        return view('hello');
    }
}
```

Update your route:

```
Route::get('/hello', [HelloController::class, 'index']);
```

Practical Exercises

1. Create a new `/about` route that displays information about you

2. Generate an `AboutController` with an `index` method

3. Create an `about.blade.php` view with basic HTML content

4. Connect everything using the techniques learned

Summary

In this chapter you've learned:

-   What Laravel is and its basic requirements

- How to install and configure a new project
- The basic structure of a Laravel project
- How to create simple routes, views, and controllers
- Basic usage of Artisan CLI

The Foundations of Modern PHP Development with Laravel

Introduction to Modern PHP Development

Before diving into Laravel, it's essential to understand how modern PHP development has evolved. Gone are the days of writing PHP scripts directly in HTML files. Today's PHP development emphasizes:

- Object-Oriented Programming (OOP)

- Design Patterns

- Dependency Management

- Automated Testing

- Security Best Practices

Laravel embodies these modern principles while making them accessible and enjoyable to use.

Understanding MVC Architecture

Laravel follows the Model-View-Controller (MVC) pattern:

```
User Request
     ↓
   Route
     ↓
Controller (Logic)
     ↓         ↘
Model (Data)   View (Display)
```

Models

- Represent your data structure

- Handle database interactions

- Define relationships

- Enforce business rules

Views

- Present data to users

- Handle layout and templating

- Separate logic from presentation

- Use Blade templating engine

Controllers

- Process user requests

- Coordinate between Models and Views

- Handle user input

- Return responses

Setting Up Your Development Environment

Modern PHP Development Tools

1. **Required Software:**

```
# Install PHP 8.1 or higher
# For Ubuntu/Debian:
sudo apt update
sudo apt install php8.1 php8.1-common php8.1-curl php8.1-mbstring php8.1-mysql php8.1-xml

# Install Composer
php -r "copy('https://getcomposer.org/installer', 'composer-setup.php');"
php composer-setup.php
sudo mv composer.phar /usr/local/bin/composer
```

2. **Development Environment Options:**

- Laravel Valet (Mac)

- Laravel Homestead (Virtual Machine)

- Docker with Laravel Sail

- XAMPP/WAMP (Basic Option)

3. **Code Editor Setup:**

```
// VSCode settings.json recommended settings
{
    "php.suggest.basic": false,
    "php.validate.enable": true,
    "php.format.rules.alignConsecutiveAssignments": true,
    "php.format.rules.spacing": true
}
```

Creating Your First Laravel Project

Project Initialization

```
# Create new project
composer create-project laravel/laravel my-first-project

# Navigate to project
cd my-first-project

# Install dependencies
composer install
```

```
# Generate application key
php artisan key:generate
```

Understanding Project Structure

```
my-first-project/
├── app/              # Application core code
│   ├── Http/         # Controllers, Middleware
│   ├── Models/       # Eloquent models
│   └── Providers/    # Service providers
├── bootstrap/        # Framework bootstrapping
├── config/           # Configuration files
├── database/         # Migrations, seeds
├── public/           # Web server entry point
├── resources/        # Frontend assets
│   ├── css/
│   ├── js/
│   └── views/        # Blade templates
├── routes/           # Route definitions
│   ├── web.php       # Web routes
│   └── api.php       # API routes
├── storage/          # Generated files
└── tests/            # Test files
```

Writing Your First Code

1. Create a Model

```php
// app/Models/Post.php
<?php

namespace App\Models;

use Illuminate\Database\Eloquent\Model;

class Post extends Model
{
    protected $fillable = [
        'title',
        'content',
        'author_id'
    ];

    public function author()
    {
        return $this->belongsTo(User::class);
    }
}
```

2. Generate Migration

```
php artisan make:migration create_posts_table
```

```php
// database/migrations/xxxx_xx_xx_create_posts_table.php
public function up()
{
```

```
    Schema::create('posts', function (Blueprint $table) {
        $table->id();
        $table->string('title');
        $table->text('content');
        $table->foreignId('author_id')->constrained('users');
        $table->timestamps();
    });
}
```

3. Create Controller

```php
// app/Http/Controllers/PostController.php
<?php

namespace App\Http\Controllers;

use App\Models\Post;
use Illuminate\Http\Request;

class PostController extends Controller
{
    public function index()
    {
        $posts = Post::with('author')->latest()->get();
        return view('posts.index', compact('posts'));
    }

    public function create()
    {
        return view('posts.create');
    }

    public function store(Request $request)
    {
        $validated = $request->validate([
            'title' => 'required|max:255',
            'content' => 'required'
        ]);

        $post = Post::create($validated);
        return redirect()->route('posts.show', $post);
    }
}
```

4. Define Routes

```php
// routes/web.php
Route::resource('posts', PostController::class);
```

5. Create Views

```php
// resources/views/posts/index.blade.php
@extends('layouts.app')

@section('content')
    <div class="container">
```

```
        <h1>Blog Posts</h1>
        @foreach($posts as $post)
            <article class="mb-4">
                <h2>{{ $post->title }}</h2>
                <p>{{ Str::limit($post->content, 200) }}</p>
                <small>By: {{ $post->author->name }}</small>
            </article>
        @endforeach
    </div>
@endsection
```

Best Practices and Common Pitfalls

Best Practices

1. **Use Dependency Injection**

```
public function__construct(
    private PostRepository $posts
) {}
```

2. **Validate Input**

```
$validated = $request->validate([
    'email' => 'required|email|unique:users',
    'password' => 'required|min:8'
]);
```

3. **Use Configuration Files**

```
// config/blog.php
return [
    'posts_per_page' => 10,
    'admin_email' => env('ADMIN_EMAIL')
];
```

Common Pitfalls

1. Not using migrations for database changes

2. Putting business logic in controllers

3. Not using Laravel's security features

4. Ignoring database indexing

Practical Exercise: Build a Simple Blog

Create a basic blog with:

1. User authentication

2. CRUD operations for posts

3. Basic commenting system

4. Simple admin panel

Summary

In this chapter, you've learned:

- The fundamentals of modern PHP development

- Laravel's basic architecture

- How to set up a development environment

- Creating your first Laravel application

- Best practices and common pitfalls

Laravel Programming Manual

1. Initial Setup

1.1 System Requirements
- **Components:**
  - PHP >= 8.1
  - Composer
  - Node.js & NPM
  - Database (MySQL/PostgreSQL)
  - Web server
  - Required PHP extensions

1.2 Installation
```
composer create-project laravel/laravel project
cd project
php artisan serve
```

2. Project Structure

2.1 Main Directories
- **app/**
  - Console/
  - Http/
  - Models/
  - Providers/
  - Services/
- **config/**
  - Configuration files
- **database/**
  - migrations/
  - seeders/
  - factories/
- **resources/**
  - views/

- o lang/

- o js/

- o css/

- **routes/**

    - o web.php

    - o api.php

    - o console.php

    - o channels.php

2.2 Key Files

- .env

- composer.json

- package.json

- artisan

- webpack.mix.js

3. Routing System

3.1 Route Definition

```
// routes/web.php
Route::get('/users', [UserController::class, 'index']);
Route::post('/users', [UserController::class, 'store']);
Route::put('/users/{id}', [UserController::class, 'update']);
Route::delete('/users/{id}', [UserController::class, 'destroy']);

// Named routes
Route::get('/profile', [ProfileController::class, 'show'])->name('profile');

// Route groups
Route::middleware(['auth'])->group(function () {
    // Protected routes
});
```

3.2 Middleware

```
// app/Http/Middleware/CheckRole.php
class CheckRole
{
    public function handle($request, Closure $next, $role)
    {
        if (!auth()->user()->hasRole($role)) {
            return redirect('home');
        }
        return $next($request);
```

```
    }
}
```

4. Controllers

4.1 Basic Structure

```php
namespace App\Http\Controllers;

class UserController extends Controller
{
    public function index()
    {
        $users = User::all();
        return view('users.index', compact('users'));
    }

    public function store(Request $request)
    {
        $validated = $request->validate([
            'name' => 'required|string|max:255',
            'email' => 'required|email|unique:users',
        ]);

        User::create($validated);
        return redirect()->route('users.index');
    }
}
```

4.2 Resource Controllers

```
php artisan make:controller UserController --resource
```

5. Models and Eloquent ORM

5.1 Model Definition

```php
namespace App\Models;

class User extends Model
{
    protected $fillable = [
        'name', 'email', 'password'
    ];

    protected $hidden = [
        'password', 'remember_token'
    ];

    // Relationships
    public function posts()
    {
        return $this->hasMany(Post::class);
    }
}
```

5.2 Common Operations

```php
// Create
User::create($data);

// Read
User::find($id);
User::where('active', 1)->get();

// Update
User::where('id', $id)->update($data);

// Delete
User::destroy($id);
```

6. Migrations and Database

6.1 Creating Migrations

```
php artisan make:migration create_users_table
```

6.2 Migration Structure

```php
public function up()
{
    Schema::create('users', function (Blueprint $table) {
        $table->id();
        $table->string('name');
        $table->string('email')->unique();
        $table->timestamp('email_verified_at')->nullable();
        $table->string('password');
        $table->rememberToken();
        $table->timestamps();
    });
}
```

7. Views and Blade

7.1 Blade Syntax

```php
// resources/views/users/index.blade.php
@extends('layouts.app')

@section('content')
    @foreach($users as $user)
        <div>
            <h2>{{ $user->name }}</h2>
            @if($user->isAdmin)
                <span>Administrator</span>
            @endif
        </div>
    @endforeach
@endsection
```

7.2 Components

```
// Blade component
<x-alert type="error" :message="$message"/>

// Component class
php artisan make:component Alert
```

8. Validation

8.1 Validation Rules

```php
$validated = $request->validate([
    'title' => 'required|unique:posts|max:255',
    'body' => 'required',
    'publish_at' => 'nullable|date',
]);
```

8.2 Form Requests

```php
php artisan make:request StoreUserRequest

class StoreUserRequest extends FormRequest
{
    public function rules()
    {
        return [
            'name' => 'required|string|max:255',
            'email' => 'required|email|unique:users',
        ];
    }
}
```

9. Authentication and Authorization

9.1 Authentication

```php
// config/auth.php
'guards' => [
    'web' => [
        'driver' => 'session',
        'provider' => 'users',
    ],
]

// Middleware
Route::middleware('auth')->group(function () {
    // Protected routes
});
```

9.2 Policies

```php
php artisan make:policy PostPolicy

class PostPolicy
{
```

```php
    public function update(User $user, Post $post)
    {
        return $user->id === $post->user_id;
    }
}
```

10. API and Resources

10.1 API Resources

```php
php artisan make:resource UserResource

class UserResource extends JsonResource
{
    public function toArray($request)
    {
        return [
            'id' => $this->id,
            'name' => $this->name,
            'email' => $this->email,
        ];
    }
}
```

10.2 API Controllers

```php
class ApiUserController extends Controller
{
    public function index()
    {
        return UserResource::collection(User::paginate());
    }

    public function show(User $user)
    {
        return new UserResource($user);
    }
}
```

11. Testing

11.1 Unit Tests

```php
public function test_user_can_be_created()
{
    $response = $this->post('/users', [
        'name' => 'Test User',
        'email' => 'test@example.com',
        'password' => 'password',
    ]);

    $response->assertStatus(201);
    $this->assertDatabaseHas('users', [
        'email' => 'test@example.com'
```

```
    ]);
}
```

11.2 Factories

```php
class UserFactory extends Factory
{
    public function definition()
    {
        return [
            'name' => $this->faker->name(),
            'email' => $this->faker->unique()->safeEmail(),
        ];
    }
}
```

12. Deployment and Optimization

12.1 Optimization

```
php artisan config:cache
php artisan route:cache
php artisan view:cache
composer install --optimize-autoloader --no-dev
```

12.2 Deployment

- Server configuration

- Environment variables

- File permissions

- Database configuration

- SSL/TLS

- Monitoring

Laravel Advanced Query Use Cases

1. E-Commerce Analytics System

1.1 Sales Analysis

```
class SalesAnalytics
{
    public function getRevenueStats($dateRange)
    {
        return Order::select([
            DB::raw('DATE(created_at) as date'),
            DB::raw('SUM(total_amount) as revenue'),
            DB::raw('COUNT(*) as orders'),
            DB::raw('AVG(total_amount) as average_order_value')
        ])
        ->whereBetween('created_at', $dateRange)
        ->groupBy('date')
        ->orderBy('date')
        ->get()
        ->map(function ($stat) {
            $stat->revenue_growth = $this->calculateGrowth($stat->revenue);
            return $stat;
        });
    }

    public function getTopSellingProducts()
    {
        return OrderItem::select([
            'product_id',
            DB::raw('SUM(quantity) as total_sold'),
            DB::raw('SUM(quantity * price) as total_revenue')
        ])
        ->with(['product:id,name,sku'])
        ->whereHas('order', function($query) {
            $query->where('status', 'completed');
        })
        ->groupBy('product_id')
        ->orderByDesc('total_revenue')
        ->limit(10)
        ->get();
    }
}
```

1.2 Customer Segmentation

```
class CustomerSegmentation
{
    public function getHighValueCustomers()
    {
        return Customer::select([
            'customers.*',
            DB::raw('COUNT(DISTINCT orders.id) as order_count'),
            DB::raw('SUM(orders.total_amount) as total_spent')
```

```
        ])
        ->leftJoin('orders', 'customers.id', '=', 'orders.customer_id')
        ->groupBy('customers.id')
        ->havingRaw('total_spent >= ?', [1000])
        ->with(['lastOrder', 'favoriteProducts'])
        ->orderByDesc('total_spent')
        ->get();
    }

    public function getChurnRiskCustomers()
    {
        $inactiveThreshold = now()->subMonths(3);

        return Customer::whereDoesntHave('orders', function($query) use
($inactiveThreshold) {
            $query->where('created_at', '>', $inactiveThreshold);
        })
        ->whereHas('orders', function($query) {
            $query->where('created_at', '<=', now()->subYear());
        })
        ->withCount('orders')
        ->withSum('orders', 'total_amount')
        ->having('orders_count', '>=', 2)
        ->get();
    }
}
```

2. Content Management System

2.1 Advanced Content Filtering

```
class ContentRepository
{
    public function getFilteredContent($filters)
    {
        return Article::query()
            ->when($filters['status'] ?? null, function($query, $status) {
                $query->where('status', $status);
            })
            ->when($filters['search'] ?? null, function($query, $search) {
                $query->where(function($q) use ($search) {
                    $q->where('title', 'like', "%{$search}%")
                        ->orWhereHas('tags', function($q) use ($search) {
                            $q->where('name', 'like', "%{$search}%");
                        });
                });
            })
            ->when($filters['category'] ?? null, function($query, $category) {
                $query->whereHas('categories', function($q) use ($category) {
                    $q->where('slug', $category);
                });
            })
            ->withCount(['comments', 'likes'])
            ->with(['author', 'categories', 'tags'])
            ->orderByDesc('published_at')
```

```
                ->paginate(15);
    }

    public function getRelatedContent($article)
    {
        return Article::where('id', '!=', $article->id)
            ->whereHas('categories', function($query) use ($article) {
                $query->whereIn('id', $article->categories->pluck('id'));
            })
            ->orWhereHas('tags', function($query) use ($article) {
                $query->whereIn('id', $article->tags->pluck('id'));
            })
            ->orderByRaw('RAND()')
            ->take(3)
            ->get();
    }
}
```

3. Real-time Dashboard Analytics

3.1 Performance Metrics

```
class DashboardMetrics
{
    public function getRealTimeStats()
    {
        return Cache::remember('dashboard.realtime', now()->addMinutes(5), function()
{
            return [
                'active_users' => $this->getActiveUsers(),
                'system_health' => $this->getSystemHealth(),
                'recent_activities' => $this->getRecentActivities()
            ];
        });
    }

    private function getActiveUsers()
    {
        return User::select([
            DB::raw('COUNT(*) as total_active'),
            DB::raw("COUNT(CASE WHEN last_activity >= NOW() - INTERVAL 5 MINUTE THEN
1 END) as last_5_min"),
            DB::raw("COUNT(CASE WHEN last_activity >= NOW() - INTERVAL 1 HOUR THEN 1
END) as last_hour")
        ])
        ->where('last_activity', '>=', now()->subDay())
        ->first();
    }

    private function getSystemHealth()
    {
        return [
            'error_rate' => ErrorLog::where('created_at', '>=', now()->subHour())
                ->select(DB::raw('COUNT(*) / 60 as error_rate'))
                ->first()->error_rate,
```

```php
            'average_response_time' => RequestLog::where('created_at', '>=', now()-
>subMinutes(5))
                ->avg('response_time'),
            'server_load' => ServerMetric::latest()->first()->load_average
        ];
    }
}
```

4. Recommendation Engine

4.1 Product Recommendations

```php
class RecommendationEngine
{
    public function getPersonalizedRecommendations($user)
    {
        $viewedProducts = $user->viewedProducts()
            ->pluck('product_id');

        $categoryPreferences = $this->getUserCategoryPreferences($user);

        return Product::whereNotIn('id', $viewedProducts)
            ->whereHas('categories', function($query) use ($categoryPreferences) {
                $query->whereIn('id', array_keys($categoryPreferences));
            })
            ->withCount(['orders', 'reviews'])
            ->orderBy(DB::raw('RAND() * (
                orders_count * 0.4 +
                reviews_count * 0.3 +
                CASE WHEN created_at >= NOW() - INTERVAL 30 DAY THEN 0.3 ELSE 0 END
            )'), 'desc')
            ->take(10)
            ->get();
    }

    private function getUserCategoryPreferences($user)
    {
        return OrderItem::select('categories.id', DB::raw('COUNT(*) as
purchase_count'))
            ->join('products', 'order_items.product_id', '=', 'products.id')
            ->join('category_product', 'products.id', '=',
'category_product.product_id')
            ->join('categories', 'category_product.category_id', '=',
'categories.id')
            ->where('order_items.user_id', $user->id)
            ->groupBy('categories.id')
            ->orderByDesc('purchase_count')
            ->pluck('purchase_count', 'id')
            ->toArray();
    }
}
```

5. Automated Reporting System

5.1 Report Generation

```php
class ReportGenerator
{
    public function generateMonthlyReport($month, $year)
    {
        $startDate = Carbon::create($year, $month, 1)->startOfMonth();
        $endDate = $startDate->copy()->endOfMonth();

        return [
            'sales' => $this->getSalesMetrics($startDate, $endDate),
            'customer_acquisition' => $this->getCustomerMetrics($startDate,
$endDate),
            'inventory' => $this->getInventoryMetrics(),
            'performance' => $this->getPerformanceMetrics($startDate, $endDate)
        ];
    }

    private function getSalesMetrics($start, $end)
    {
        return Order::select([
            DB::raw('SUM(total_amount) as total_revenue'),
            DB::raw('AVG(total_amount) as average_order_value'),
            DB::raw('COUNT(*) as total_orders'),
            DB::raw('COUNT(DISTINCT customer_id) as unique_customers')
        ])
        ->whereBetween('created_at', [$start, $end])
        ->where('status', 'completed')
        ->first()
        ->toArray();
    }
}
```

Laravel Eloquent Relationships Guide

1. One To One Relationships

1.1 Basic Definition

```
class User extends Model
{
    // HasOne relationship
    public function profile()
    {
        return $this->hasOne(Profile::class);
    }
}

class Profile extends Model
{
    // Inverse of the relationship
    public function user()
    {
        return $this->belongsTo(User::class);
    }
}
```

1.2 Advanced One To One

```
// Custom foreign key
public function profile()
{
    return $this->hasOne(Profile::class, 'custom_user_id');
}

// Custom local key
public function profile()
{
    return $this->hasOne(Profile::class, 'user_id', 'custom_id');
}

// With constraints
public function activeProfile()
{
    return $this->hasOne(Profile::class)->where('active', true);
}
```

2. One To Many Relationships

2.1 Basic Definition

```
class User extends Model
{
    // HasMany relationship
    public function posts()
    {
        return $this->hasMany(Post::class);
    }
}
```

```
    }
}

class Post extends Model
{
    public function user()
    {
        return $this->belongsTo(User::class);
    }
}
```

2.2 Advanced Usage

```
// With constraints
public function recentPosts()
{
    return $this->hasMany(Post::class)
        ->orderBy('created_at', 'desc')
        ->take(5);
}

// With count
public function posts()
{
    return $this->hasMany(Post::class)
        ->withCount('comments');
}
```

3. Many To Many Relationships

3.1 Basic Definition

```
class User extends Model
{
    public function roles()
    {
        return $this->belongsToMany(Role::class);
    }
}

class Role extends Model
{
    public function users()
    {
        return $this->belongsToMany(User::class);
    }
}
```

3.2 Advanced Many To Many

```
// With pivot table customization
public function roles()
{
    return $this->belongsToMany(Role::class)
        ->withPivot('active', 'created_by')
        ->withTimestamps();
```

```php
}

// Custom intermediate table and foreign keys
public function roles()
{
    return $this->belongsToMany(Role::class,
        'user_role_table',
        'user_id',
        'role_id'
    );
}
```

4. Has One Through & Has Many Through

4.1 Has One Through

```php
class Mechanic extends Model
{
    public function carOwner()
    {
        return $this->hasOneThrough(
            Owner::class,
            Car::class,
            'mechanic_id', // Foreign key on cars table
            'car_id',      // Foreign key on owners table
            'id',          // Local key on mechanics table
            'id'           // Local key on cars table
        );
    }
}
```

4.2 Has Many Through

```php
class Country extends Model
{
    public function posts()
    {
        return $this->hasManyThrough(
            Post::class,
            User::class,
            'country_id', // Foreign key on users table
            'user_id',    // Foreign key on posts table
            'id',         // Local key on countries table
            'id'          // Local key on users table
        );
    }
}
```

5. Polymorphic Relationships

5.1 One To One Polymorphic

```php
class Image extends Model
{
    public function imageable()
```

```
    {
        return $this->morphTo();
    }
}

class User extends Model
{
    public function image()
    {
        return $this->morphOne(Image::class, 'imageable');
    }
}
```

5.2 One To Many Polymorphic

```
class Comment extends Model
{
    public function commentable()
    {
        return $this->morphTo();
    }
}

class Post extends Model
{
    public function comments()
    {
        return $this->morphMany(Comment::class, 'commentable');
    }
}
```

6. Querying Relationships

6.1 Eager Loading

```
// Basic eager loading
$users = User::with('posts')->get();

// Multiple relationships
$users = User::with(['posts', 'profile'])->get();

// Nested relationships
$users = User::with('posts.comments')->get();

// Lazy eager loading
$users = User::all();
$users->load('posts');
```

6.2 Constraining Eager Loads

```
$users = User::with(['posts' => function ($query) {
    $query->where('active', true)
        ->orderBy('created_at', 'desc');
}])->get();

// Count related models
```

```
$users = User::withCount(['posts' => function ($query) {
    $query->where('active', true);
}])->get();
```

7. Relationship Methods vs. Dynamic Properties

7.1 Method Access

```
// Relationship as method
$user->posts()->where('active', true)->get();

// Create related model
$user->posts()->create([
    'title' => 'New Post'
]);

// Save with custom attributes
$post = new Post(['title' => 'New Post']);
$user->posts()->save($post, ['additional_data' => 'value']);
```

7.2 Dynamic Properties

```
// Accessing as property
$user->posts; // Returns collection of posts

// Checking for existence
if ($user->posts->count() > 0) {
    // User has posts
}

// Iterating
foreach ($user->posts as $post) {
    echo $post->title;
}
```

Advanced Querying Techniques in Laravel

1. Advanced Eloquent Queries

1.1 Subqueries

```
// Using subqueries in selects
$users = User::select([
    'users.*',
    'last_post' => Post::select('title')
        ->whereColumn('user_id', 'users.id')
        ->latest()
        ->limit(1)
])->get();

// Subqueries in where clauses
$users = User::where(function($query) {
    $query->select('type')
        ->from('profiles')
        ->whereColumn('user_id', 'users.id')
        ->where('active', true)
        ->limit(1);
}, 'premium')->get();
```

1.2 Advanced Joins

```
// Join with subqueries
$users = User::joinSub(
    Post::select('user_id')
        ->groupBy('user_id')
        ->havingRaw('COUNT(*) > ?', [3]),
    'active_users',
    'users.id',
    '=',
    'active_users.user_id'
)->get();

// Conditional joins
$users = User::leftJoin('profiles', function($join) {
    $join->on('users.id', '=', 'profiles.user_id')
        ->where('profiles.active', '=', true);
})->get();
```

2. Complex Aggregations

2.1 Aggregation Functions

```
// Multiple aggregations
$statistics = User::select([
    DB::raw('COUNT(*) as total'),
    DB::raw('AVG(age) as average_age'),
    DB::raw('SUM(CASE WHEN active = 1 THEN 1 ELSE 0 END) as active_users')
])->first();
```

```
// Conditional aggregations
$results = Post::select('category')
    ->selectRaw('COUNT(*) as total')
    ->selectRaw('SUM(CASE WHEN likes > 100 THEN 1 ELSE 0 END) as popular')
    ->groupBy('category')
    ->having('total', '>', 10)
    ->get();
```

2.2 Window Functions

```
// Window functions
$rankings = Post::select([
    'category',
    'title',
    'views',
    DB::raw('RANK() OVER (PARTITION BY category ORDER BY views DESC) as ranking')
])->get();

// Cumulative calculations
$trends = Post::select([
    'date',
    'views',
    DB::raw('SUM(views) OVER (ORDER BY date) as cumulative_views')
])->get();
```

3. Advanced Relationship Queries

3.1 Has and WhereHas

```
// Complex nested queries
$users = User::whereHas('posts', function($query) {
    $query->where('active', true)
        ->whereHas('comments', function($q) {
            $q->where('approved', true)
                ->where('created_at', '>=', now()->subDays(7));
        }, '>=', 3);
}, '>=', 5)->get();

// Combining Has and WhereHas
$users = User::has('posts', '>=', 3)
    ->whereHas('profile', function($query) {
        $query->where('verified', true);
    })
    ->with(['posts' => function($query) {
        $query->latest()->take(5);
    }])
    ->get();
```

3.2 Exists and WhereExists

```
// Existence queries
$users = User::whereExists(function($query) {
    $query->select(DB::raw(1))
        ->from('profiles')
        ->whereColumn('profiles.user_id', 'users.id')
        ->where('level', 'premium');
```

```
})->get();

// Non-existence queries
$inactive = User::whereDoesntHave('sessions', function($query) {
    $query->where('last_activity', '>=', now()->subDays(30));
})->get();
```

4. Advanced Sorting and Filtering

4.1 Custom Ordering
```
// Order by relationship
$users = User::withCount('posts')
    ->orderBy('posts_count', 'desc')
    ->orderBy(
        Post::select('created_at')
            ->whereColumn('user_id', 'users.id')
            ->latest()
            ->limit(1)
    )
    ->get();

// Custom field ordering
$posts = Post::orderByRaw('FIELD(status, "featured", "active", "draft")')
    ->orderBy('created_at', 'desc')
    ->get();
```

4.2 Dynamic Filters
```
class PostQuery extends Builder
{
    public function filter(array $filters)
    {
        return $this->when($filters['search'] ?? null, function($query, $search) {
            $query->where(function($q) use ($search) {
                $q->where('title', 'like', "%{$search}%")
                    ->orWhere('content', 'like', "%{$search}%");
            });
        })->when($filters['category'] ?? null, function($query, $category) {
            $query->where('category_id', $category);
        })->when($filters['date'] ?? null, function($query, $date) {
            $query->whereDate('created_at', $date);
        });
    }
}
```

5. Query Optimization

5.1 Efficient Queries
```
// Select specific fields
$users = User::select(['id', 'name', 'email'])
    ->with(['profile' => function($query) {
        $query->select(['id', 'user_id', 'bio']);
    }])
```

```
    ->get();

// Use chunking for large sets
User::chunk(1000, function($users) {
    foreach ($users as $user) {
        // Process user
    }
});
```

5.2 Query Caching

```
// Cache results
$users = Cache::remember('users.active', now()->addHours(24), function() {
    return User::where('active', true)
        ->with('profile')
        ->get();
});

// Cache with tags
Cache::tags(['users', 'reports'])->remember('statistics', now()->addDay(), function()
{
    return User::selectRaw('COUNT(*) as total, SUM(active) as active')
        ->first();
});
```

6. Real-time Queries

6.1 Query Scopes

```
// Dynamic scopes
class User extends Model
{
    public function scopeRecentActivity($query, $days = 7)
    {
        return $query->whereHas('sessions', function($q) use ($days) {
            $q->where('last_activity', '>=', now()->subDays($days));
        });
    }
}

// Usage
$activeUsers = User::recentActivity(30)->get();
```

6.2 Event-based Queries

```
// Real-time event queries
class PostObserver
{
    public function created(Post $post)
    {
        Cache::tags('posts')->flush();

        $statistics = Post::selectRaw('
            COUNT(*) as total,
            AVG(CASE WHEN created_at >= ? THEN likes ELSE 0 END) as
average_recent_likes
```

```
        ', [now()->subDays(7)])->first();

        Cache::put('statistics.posts', $statistics, now()->addDay());
    }
}
```

Laravel Recommendation Algorithms

1. Collaborative-Based Recommendation

1.1 User-User Collaborative Filtering

```
class CollaborativeRecommendation
{
    public function getRecommendationsBySimilarUsers($user_id)
    {
        return Cache::remember("recommendations.user.{$user_id}", now()-
>addHours(12), function() use ($user_id) {
            // Get current user's purchase history
            $userPurchases = Purchase::where('user_id', $user_id)
                ->pluck('product_id')
                ->toArray();

            // Find similar users
            $similarUsers = User::whereHas('purchases', function($query) use
($userPurchases) {
                $query->whereIn('product_id', $userPurchases);
            })
            ->withCount(['purchases' => function($query) use ($userPurchases) {
                $query->whereIn('product_id', $userPurchases);
            }])
            ->having('purchases_count', '>=', 3)
            ->orderByDesc('purchases_count')
            ->take(10)
            ->pluck('id');

            // Get products purchased by similar users
            return Product::whereHas('purchases', function($query) use
($similarUsers, $userPurchases) {
                $query->whereIn('user_id', $similarUsers)
                    ->whereNotIn('product_id', $userPurchases);
            })
            ->withCount(['purchases' => function($query) use ($similarUsers) {
                $query->whereIn('user_id', $similarUsers);
            }])
            ->orderByDesc('purchases_count')
            ->take(10)
            ->get();
        });
    }
}
```

1.2 Item-Item Collaborative Filtering

```
class ItemBasedRecommendation
{
    public function getRelatedProducts($product_id)
    {
        $similarityMatrix = Cache::remember("similarity.product.{$product_id}",
now()->addDay(), function() use ($product_id) {
```

```php
            // Get users who bought this product
            $buyerUsers = Purchase::where('product_id', $product_id)
                ->pluck('user_id');

            // Find other products bought by these users
            return Product::whereHas('purchases', function($query) use ($buyerUsers)
{

                $query->whereIn('user_id', $buyerUsers);
            })
            ->withCount(['purchases' => function($query) use ($buyerUsers) {
                $query->whereIn('user_id', $buyerUsers);
            }])
            ->where('id', '!=', $product_id)
            ->orderByDesc('purchases_count')
            ->take(10)
            ->get();
        });

        return $similarityMatrix;
    }
}
```

2. Content-Based Recommendation

2.1 Feature Analysis

```php
class ContentBasedRecommendation
{
    public function getRecommendationsByFeatures($product_id)
    {
        $product = Product::with(['categories', 'tags', 'attributes'])-
>find($product_id);

        return Product::where('id', '!=', $product_id)
            ->where(function($query) use ($product) {
                // Category matching
                $query->whereHas('categories', function($q) use ($product) {
                    $q->whereIn('id', $product->categories->pluck('id'));
                }, '>=', 2);

                // Tag matching
                $query->orWhereHas('tags', function($q) use ($product) {
                    $q->whereIn('name', $product->tags->pluck('name'));
                }, '>=', 3);

                // Price range matching
                $query->whereBetween('price', [
                    $product->price * 0.8,
                    $product->price * 1.2
                ]);
            })
            ->withCount(['categories' => function($query) use ($product) {
                $query->whereIn('id', $product->categories->pluck('id'));
            }])
            ->orderByDesc('categories_count')
```

```
            ->take(10)
            ->get();
    }
}
```

3. Hybrid Recommendation

3.1 Method Combination

```
class HybridRecommendation
{
    protected $collaborative;
    protected $contentBased;

    public function __construct(
        CollaborativeRecommendation $collaborative,
        ContentBasedRecommendation $contentBased
    ) {
        $this->collaborative = $collaborative;
        $this->contentBased = $contentBased;
    }

    public function getHybridRecommendations($user_id, $product_id = null)
    {
        // Get recommendations from both methods
        $collaborativeRecommendations = collect($this->collaborative
            ->getRecommendationsBySimilarUsers($user_id));

        $contentBasedRecommendations = collect($product_id ?
            $this->contentBased->getRecommendationsByFeatures($product_id) :
            collect([]));

        // Combine and weight results
        $combinedRecommendations = $collaborativeRecommendations
            ->concat($contentBasedRecommendations)
            ->groupBy('id')
            ->map(function($group) {
                $product = $group->first();
                $product->score = $this->calculateScore($group);
                return $product;
            })
            ->sortByDesc('score')
            ->values()
            ->take(10);

        return $combinedRecommendations;
    }

    private function calculateScore($group)
    {
        return (
            ($group->count() > 1 ? 1.5 : 1) * // Bonus if appears in both methods
            ($group->sum('relevance') / $group->count()) // Average relevance
        );
```

```
        }
}
```

4. Contextual Recommendation

4.1 Time-Based Context

```
class ContextualRecommendation
{
    public function getContextualRecommendations($user_id)
    {
        $hour = now()->hour;
        $dayOfWeek = now()->dayOfWeek;
        $season = $this->determineSeason();

        return Product::query()
            ->when($hour >= 11 && $hour <= 14, function($query) {
                // Popular lunch time products
                $query->whereHas('categories', function($q) {
                    $q->where('name', 'like', '%food%');
                });
            })
            ->when($dayOfWeek >= 1 && $dayOfWeek <= 5, function($query) {
                // Popular weekday products
                $query->where('type', 'productivity');
            })
            ->when($season, function($query, $season) {
                // Seasonal products
                $query->whereHas('tags', function($q) use ($season) {
                    $q->where('name', $season);
                });
            })
            ->withCount(['purchases' => function($query) {
                $query->whereRaw('HOUR(created_at) = ?', [now()->hour])
                    ->whereRaw('DAYOFWEEK(created_at) = ?', [now()->dayOfWeek]);
            }])
            ->orderByDesc('purchases_count')
            ->take(10)
            ->get();
    }

    private function determineSeason()
    {
        $month = now()->month;
        return match(true) {
            in_array($month, [12, 1, 2]) => 'winter',
            in_array($month, [3, 4, 5]) => 'spring',
            in_array($month, [6, 7, 8]) => 'summer',
            default => 'fall'
        };
    }
}
```

5. Continuous Learning System

5.1 Feedback and Improvement

```
class RecommendationLearning
{
    public function recordInteraction(User $user, Product $product, $type)
    {
        UserInteraction::create([
            'user_id' => $user->id,
            'product_id' => $product->id,
            'type' => $type,
            'context' => [
                'hour' => now()->hour,
                'day_of_week' => now()->dayOfWeek,
                'device' => request()->header('User-Agent'),
                'location' => request()->ip()
            ]
        ]);

        // Update recommendation scores
        $this->updateProductScores($product->id);
    }

    private function updateProductScores($product_id)
    {
        $scores = UserInteraction::where('product_id', $product_id)
            ->selectRaw('
                SUM(CASE
                    WHEN type = "purchase" THEN 5
                    WHEN type = "view" THEN 1
                    WHEN type = "favorite" THEN 3
                    ELSE 0
                END) as total_score,
                COUNT(*) as total_interactions
            ')
            ->first();

        ProductScore::updateOrCreate(
            ['product_id' => $product_id],
            [
                'score' => $scores->total_score / $scores->total_interactions,
                'last_update' => now()
            ]
        );
    }
}
```

External API Integration for Recommendation Systems

1. OpenAI Integration

1.1 Natural Language Based Recommendations

```php
class OpenAIRecommender
{
    protected $client;

    public function __construct()
    {
        $this->client = OpenAI::client(config('services.openai.api_key'));
    }

    public function getPersonalizedRecommendations($user_id)
    {
        $user = User::with(['history', 'preferences'])->find($user_id);

        $prompt = $this->buildPrompt($user);

        try {
            $response = $this->client->chat()->create([
                'model' => 'gpt-4',
                'messages' => [
                    [
                        'role' => 'system',
                        'content' => 'You are an expert recommendation system'
                    ],
                    [
                        'role' => 'user',
                        'content' => $prompt
                    ]
                ],
                'temperature' => 0.7
            ]);

            $recommendations = $this->processOpenAIResponse($response);

            return Product::whereIn('category', $recommendations)
                ->whereNotIn('id', $user->history->pluck('product_id'))
                ->take(10)
                ->get();
        } catch (\Exception $e) {
            Log::error('OpenAI Error: ' . $e->getMessage());
            return $this->getBackupRecommendations($user);
        }
    }

    protected function buildPrompt($user)
    {
        return "Based on the following user profile:
                - Interests: " . implode(', ', $user->preferences->interests) . "
```

```
                      - Purchase history: " . $user->history->pluck('name')->implode(', ')
 . "
                      - Budget: " . $user->preferences->budget . "
                      Suggest 5 relevant product categories.";
    }
}
```

2. Google Cloud AI Integration

2.1 Behavior Analysis with Vertex AI

```
class GoogleAIRecommender
{
    protected $predictionClient;
    protected $modelPath;

    public function __construct()
    {
        $this->predictionClient = new PredictionServiceClient([
            'credentials' => json_decode(
                file_get_contents(config('services.google.credentials_path')),
                true
            )
        ]);

        $this->modelPath = "projects/" . config('services.google.project_id') .
                    "/locations/us-central1/models/" .
                    config('services.google.model_id');
    }

    public function predictInterests($user_id)
    {
        $user = User::with(['behavior', 'demographics'])->find($user_id);

        try {
            $instance = $this->prepareUserData($user);

            $response = $this->predictionClient->predict([
                'name' => $this->modelPath,
                'payload' => ['instances' => [$instance]]
            ]);

            return $this->processPredictions($response->getPredictions());
        } catch (\Exception $e) {
            Log::error('Google AI Error: ' . $e->getMessage());
            return $this->getDefaultInterests($user);
        }
    }

    protected function prepareUserData($user)
    {
        return [
            'session_time' => $user->behavior->average_session_time,
            'most_visited_category' => $user->behavior->main_category,
            'age' => $user->demographics->age,
```

```
                'location' => $user->demographics->city,
                'device' => $user->behavior->main_device
        ];
    }
}
```

3. AWS Personalize Integration

3.1 Real-time Recommendations

```
class AWSPersonalizeRecommender
{
    protected $personalizeRuntime;
    protected $campaignArn;

    public function __construct()
    {
        $this->personalizeRuntime = new PersonalizeRuntimeClient([
            'version' => 'latest',
            'region' => config('services.aws.region'),
            'credentials' => [
                'key'    => config('services.aws.key'),
                'secret' => config('services.aws.secret')
            ]
        ]);

        $this->campaignArn = config('services.aws.personalize_campaign_arn');
    }

    public function getRealTimeRecommendations($user_id)
    {
        try {
            $result = $this->personalizeRuntime->getRecommendations([
                'campaignArn' => $this->campaignArn,
                'userId' => $user_id
            ]);

            return $this->processAWSRecommendations($result['itemList']);
        } catch (AwsException $e) {
            Log::error('AWS Personalize Error: ' . $e->getMessage());
            return $this->getCachedRecommendations($user_id);
        }
    }

    protected function processAWSRecommendations($itemList)
    {
        $productIds = collect($itemList)->pluck('itemId');

        return Product::whereIn('id', $productIds)
            ->with(['category', 'price', 'ratings'])
            ->get()
            ->sortBy(function($product) use ($productIds) {
                return array_search($product->id, $productIds->toArray());
            });
```

```
        }
}
```

4. Azure Cognitive Services Integration

4.1 Personalized Content Analysis

```
class AzureRecommender
{
    protected $client;
    protected $endpoint;

    public function __construct()
    {
        $this->client = new Client();
        $this->endpoint = config('services.azure.cognitive_endpoint');
    }

    public function analyzeVisualPreferences($user_id)
    {
        $user = User::with(['visualInteractions'])->find($user_id);
        $images = $user->visualInteractions->pluck('image_url');

        try {
            $results = collect($images)->map(function($image) {
                $response = $this->client->post($this->endpoint .
'/vision/v3.2/analyze', [
                    'headers' => [
                        'Ocp-Apim-Subscription-Key' =>
config('services.azure.api_key'),
                        'Content-Type' => 'application/json'
                    ],
                    'json' => [
                        'url' => $image,
                        'visualFeatures' => 'Categories,Tags,Description,Color'
                    ]
                ]);

                return json_decode($response->getBody());
            });

            return $this->generateVisualRecommendations($results);
        } catch (\Exception $e) {
            Log::error('Azure Error: ' . $e->getMessage());
            return $this->getCachedVisualRecommendations($user_id);
        }
    }

    protected function generateVisualRecommendations($analysisResults)
    {
        $preferences = $this->extractVisualPreferences($analysisResults);

        return Product::whereHas('features', function($query) use ($preferences) {
            $query->whereIn('attribute', $preferences->pluck('tag'))
                ->where('relevance', '>', 0.7);
```

```
        })
        ->with(['images', 'details'])
        ->orderBy('popularity', 'desc')
        ->take(10)
        ->get();
    }
}
```

5. Fallback and Cache System

5.1 Error Handling and Optimization

```
class HybridRecommendationSystem
{
    protected $apis = [
        OpenAIRecommender::class,
        GoogleAIRecommender::class,
        AWSPersonalizeRecommender::class,
        AzureRecommender::class
    ];

    public function getOptimizedRecommendations($user_id)
    {
        return Cache::remember("recommendations.{$user_id}", now()->addHours(2),
function() use ($user_id) {
            foreach ($this->apis as $api) {
                try {
                    $recommender = new $api();
                    $results = $recommender-
>getPersonalizedRecommendations($user_id);

                    if ($results->isNotEmpty()) {
                        return $results;
                    }
                } catch (\Exception $e) {
                    Log::warning("API Failure {$api}: " . $e->getMessage());
                    continue;
                }
            }

            return $this->getBasicRecommendations($user_id);
        });
    }

    protected function getBasicRecommendations($user_id)
    {
        return Product::withCount('sales')
            ->orderBy('sales_count', 'desc')
            ->take(10)
            ->get();
    }
}
```

Industry-Specific Recommendation Systems in Laravel

1. E-Learning Platform

1.1 Course Recommendations

```php
class LearningRecommendationEngine
{
    public function getPersonalizedCourseRecommendations($student_id)
    {
        $student = Student::with(['completedCourses', 'interests', 'skillLevel'])-
>find($student_id);

        return Course::query()
            ->whereNotIn('id', $student->completedCourses->pluck('id'))
            ->where(function($query) use ($student) {
                // Match skill level
                $query->whereBetween('difficulty_level', [
                    max(1, $student->skillLevel - 1),
                    min(10, $student->skillLevel + 2)
                ]);

                // Match learning path
                $query->whereHas('prerequisites', function($q) use ($student) {
                    $q->whereIn('id', $student->completedCourses->pluck('id'));
                });

                // Match interests
                $query->orWhereHas('tags', function($q) use ($student) {
                    $q->whereIn('name', $student->interests->pluck('name'));
                });
            })
            ->withCount(['enrollments', 'completions'])
            ->orderByRaw('(completions_count / enrollments_count) DESC')
            ->take(5)
            ->get();
    }

    public function getNextLessonRecommendation($student_id, $course_id)
    {
        return Cache::remember("next_lesson.{$student_id}.{$course_id}", now()-
>addHours(1), function() use ($student_id, $course_id) {
            $student = Student::with(['completedLessons'])->find($student_id);

            return Lesson::where('course_id', $course_id)
                ->whereNotIn('id', $student->completedLessons->pluck('id'))
                ->orderBy('sequence')
                ->first();
        });
    }
}
```

2. Healthcare Platform

2.1 Medical Resource Recommendations

```
class HealthcareRecommendationSystem
{
    public function getPersonalizedHealthContent($patient_id)
    {
        $patient = Patient::with(['conditions', 'medications', 'preferences'])-
>find($patient_id);

        return HealthArticle::query()
            ->where(function($query) use ($patient) {
                // Match medical conditions
                $query->whereHas('conditions', function($q) use ($patient) {
                    $q->whereIn('id', $patient->conditions->pluck('id'));
                });

                // Match treatment types
                $query->orWhereHas('treatments', function($q) use ($patient) {
                    $q->whereIn('medication_id', $patient->medications->pluck('id'));
                });
            })
            ->where('reading_level', '<=', $patient->preferences->reading_level)
            ->whereHas('approvals', function($q) {
                $q->where('approved', true)
                    ->where('approval_level', 'medical_board');
            })
            ->orderBy('published_at', 'desc')
            ->take(10)
            ->get();
    }

    public function getEmergencyResourceRecommendations($location, $condition_id)
    {
        return HealthcareFacility::query()
            ->select([
                'healthcare_facilities.*',
                DB::raw('ST_Distance(location, ST_GeomFromText(?, 4326)) as
distance'),
            ])
            ->addBinding($location, 'select')
            ->whereHas('specialties', function($query) use ($condition_id) {
                $query->where('condition_id', $condition_id);
            })
            ->where('is_active', true)
            ->orderBy('distance')
            ->take(5)
            ->get();
    }
}
```

3. Financial Services

3.1 Investment Product Recommendations

```php
class FinancialRecommendationEngine
{
    public function getInvestmentRecommendations($investor_id)
    {
        $investor = Investor::with(['riskProfile', 'portfolio', 'goals'])-
>find($investor_id);

        return InvestmentProduct::query()
            ->where(function($query) use ($investor) {
                // Match risk tolerance
                $query->whereBetween('risk_level', [
                    max(1, $investor->riskProfile->level - 1),
                    min(10, $investor->riskProfile->level + 1)
                ]);

                // Portfolio diversification
                $query->whereNotIn('asset_class',
                    $investor->portfolio->getOverweightedAssetClasses()
                );

                // Match investment goals
                $query->whereHas('attributes', function($q) use ($investor) {
                    $q->whereIn('goal_type', $investor->goals->pluck('type'));
                });
            })
            ->where('minimum_investment', '<=', $investor->available_funds)
            ->withCount('currentInvestors')
            ->orderByDesc('historical_performance')
            ->take(5)
            ->get();
    }
}
```

4. Media Streaming Platform

4.1 Content Recommendations

```php
class StreamingRecommendationEngine
{
    public function getPersonalizedContent($viewer_id)
    {
        $viewer = Viewer::with(['watchHistory', 'preferences'])->find($viewer_id);
        $timeOfDay = now()->hour;

        return Content::query()
            ->where(function($query) use ($viewer) {
                // Genre preferences
                $query->whereHas('genres', function($q) use ($viewer) {
                    $q->whereIn('id', $viewer->preferences->favorite_genres);
                });
```

```php
                // Content length preferences
                $query->where('duration', '<=', $viewer->preferences->max_duration);
            })
            ->where(function($query) use ($timeOfDay) {
                // Time-based recommendations
                if ($timeOfDay >= 20 || $timeOfDay <= 4) {
                    $query->where('content_type', 'movie')
                            ->orWhere('is_binge_worthy', true);
                } else {
                    $query->where('duration', '<=', 30);
                }
            })
            ->whereNotIn('id', $viewer->watchHistory->pluck('content_id'))
            ->withCount(['views', 'completions'])
            ->orderByRaw('(completions_count / views_count) DESC')
            ->take(10)
            ->get();
    }
}
```

5. Real Estate Platform

5.1 Property Recommendations

```php
class RealEstateRecommendationSystem
{
    public function getPersonalizedListings($user_id)
    {
        $user = User::with(['preferences', 'searchHistory', 'savedProperties'])-
>find($user_id);

        return Property::query()
            ->where(function($query) use ($user) {
                // Price range
                $query->whereBetween('price', [
                    $user->preferences->min_price,
                    $user->preferences->max_price
                ]);

                // Location preferences
                $query->whereHas('location', function($q) use ($user) {
                    $q->whereIn('area_id', $user->preferences->preferred_areas);
                });

                // Property features
                $query->whereHas('features', function($q) use ($user) {
                    $q->whereIn('feature_id', $user->preferences-
>must_have_features);
                });
            })
            ->where('status', 'active')
            ->whereNotIn('id', $user->viewedProperties->pluck('id'))
            ->withCount('viewings')
            ->orderBy(DB::raw('
                CASE
```

```
                WHEN price_change_date >= NOW() - INTERVAL 7 DAY THEN 1
                WHEN listed_date >= NOW() - INTERVAL 3 DAY THEN 2
                ELSE 3
            END
        '))
        ->orderByDesc('viewings_count')
        ->take(10)
        ->get();
    }
}
```

Monitoring System Optimization

1. Performance Optimization

1.1 Metric Collection Strategy

```php
class OptimizedMetricCollector
{
    protected $batchSize = 100;
    protected $flushInterval = 60; // seconds
    protected $metrics = [];

    public function collect($metric)
    {
        $this->metrics[] = [
            'name' => $metric['name'],
            'value' => $metric['value'],
            'tags' => $metric['tags'],
            'timestamp' => microtime(true)
        ];

        if (count($this->metrics) >= $this->batchSize) {
            $this->flush();
        }
    }

    protected function flush()
    {
        Redis::pipeline(function($pipe) {
            foreach ($this->metrics as $metric) {
                $key = "metrics:{$metric['name']}:" . floor($metric['timestamp']);
                $pipe->zadd($key, $metric['value'], json_encode($metric));
                $pipe->expire($key, 3600); // 1 hour retention
            }
        });

        $this->metrics = [];
    }

    public function aggregateHourlyMetrics()
    {
        return Redis::pipeline(function($pipe) {
            $hourAgo = floor(time() / 3600) * 3600;

            foreach (['response_time', 'quality_score', 'conversion_rate'] as $metricName) {
                $pipe->zrangebyscore("metrics:{$metricName}:{$hourAgo}", '-inf', '+inf');
            }
        });
    }
}
```

1.2 Resource Usage Optimization

```php
class ResourceOptimizer
{
    public function optimizeMonitoring()
    {
        return [
            'memory' => $this->optimizeMemoryUsage(),
            'cpu' => $this->optimizeCPUUsage(),
            'io' => $this->optimizeIOOperations()
        ];
    }

    protected function optimizeMemoryUsage()
    {
        $config = [
            'max_metrics_buffer' => 1000,
            'cleanup_interval' => 300,
            'compression' => true,
            'sampling_rate' => $this->calculateOptimalSamplingRate()
        ];

        if (memory_get_usage() > 512 * 1024 * 1024) { // 512MB
            $this->triggerEmergencyCleanup();
        }

        return $config;
    }

    protected function calculateOptimalSamplingRate()
    {
        $currentLoad = sys_getloadavg()[0];
        $baseRate = 1.0;

        if ($currentLoad > 2.0) {
            return min(0.1, $baseRate / log($currentLoad));
        }

        return $baseRate;
    }
}
```

2. Storage Optimization

2.1 Data Retention Strategy

```php
class DataRetentionManager
{
    protected $retentionPolicies = [
        'raw_metrics' => '24h',
        'hourly_aggregates' => '7d',
        'daily_aggregates' => '90d',
        'monthly_aggregates' => '365d'
    ];
```

```php
    public function applyRetentionPolicies()
    {
        foreach ($this->retentionPolicies as $metricType => $retention) {
            $this->cleanupOldData($metricType, $this->parseRetention($retention));
        }
    }

    protected function cleanupOldData($metricType, $retentionSeconds)
    {
        $cutoffTime = time() - $retentionSeconds;

        DB::table('metrics')
            ->where('type', $metricType)
            ->where('timestamp', '<', $cutoffTime)
            ->chunkById(1000, function($metrics) {
                foreach ($metrics as $metric) {
                    $this->archiveMetricIfNeeded($metric);
                }
            });
    }

    protected function archiveMetricIfNeeded($metric)
    {
        if ($this->isImportantMetric($metric)) {
            $this->moveToLongTermStorage($metric);
        }
    }
}
```

3. Query Optimization

3.1 Efficient Data Access

```php
class MetricsQueryOptimizer
{
    protected $cache;
    protected $indexedFields = ['timestamp', 'metric_name', 'user_id'];

    public function optimizeQuery($query)
    {
        $fingerprint = $this->generateQueryFingerprint($query);

        return Cache::remember("query:$fingerprint", 300, function() use ($query) {
            return $this->executeOptimizedQuery($query);
        });
    }

    protected function executeOptimizedQuery($query)
    {
        // Add query hints
        $query->withHint('readPreference', ['mode' => 'secondaryPreferred']);

        // Use covering indexes when possible
        foreach ($this->indexedFields as $field) {
            if ($query->hasWhere($field)) {
```

```
                    $query->forceIndex($field . '_idx');
            }
        }

        return $query->get();
    }

    protected function generateQueryFingerprint($query)
    {
        return md5(serialize([
            'conditions' => $query->getWheres(),
            'order' => $query->getOrders(),
            'limit' => $query->getLimit()
        ]));
    }
}
```

4. Alert Processing Optimization

4.1 Alert Aggregation and Deduplication

```
class AlertProcessor
{
    protected $alertBuffer = [];
    protected $processingInterval = 30; // seconds
    protected $similarityThreshold = 0.85;

    public function processAlert($alert)
    {
        if ($this->isDuplicate($alert)) {
            $this->updateExistingAlert($alert);
            return;
        }

        $this->alertBuffer[] = [
            'signature' => $this->generateAlertSignature($alert),
            'count' => 1,
            'first_seen' => time(),
            'last_seen' => time(),
            'data' => $alert
        ];

        if ($this->shouldProcessBuffer()) {
            $this->processAlertBuffer();
        }
    }

    protected function isDuplicate($alert)
    {
        $signature = $this->generateAlertSignature($alert);

        foreach ($this->alertBuffer as $bufferedAlert) {
            if (similar_text($signature, $bufferedAlert['signature']) >= $this-
>similarityThreshold) {
                return true;
```

```
                }
            }

            return false;
        }

    protected function processAlertBuffer()
    {
        $groupedAlerts = $this->groupSimilarAlerts();

        foreach ($groupedAlerts as $group) {
            if ($group['count'] > 1) {
                $this->sendAggregatedAlert($group);
            } else {
                $this->sendSingleAlert($group['data']);
            }
        }

        $this->alertBuffer = [];
    }
}
```

5. System Health Checks

5.1 Health Monitor Optimization

```
class OptimizedHealthMonitor
{
    protected $healthChecks = [];
    protected $checkResults = [];
    protected $lastCheckTime = [];

    public function registerHealthCheck($name, callable $check, $interval)
    {
        $this->healthChecks[$name] = [
            'check' => $check,
            'interval' => $interval
        ];
    }

    public function runHealthChecks()
    {
        $currentTime = time();

        foreach ($this->healthChecks as $name => $check) {
            if (!isset($this->lastCheckTime[$name]) ||
                ($currentTime - $this->lastCheckTime[$name]) >= $check['interval']) {

                try {
                    $this->checkResults[$name] = [
                        'status' => $check['check'](),
                        'timestamp' => $currentTime
                    ];
                    $this->lastCheckTime[$name] = $currentTime;
                } catch (\Exception $e) {
```

```php
                Log::error("Health check failed for {$name}: " . $e-
>getMessage());
            }
        }
    }

    return $this->checkResults;
    }
}
```

Error Handling and Fallback Strategies

1. Comprehensive Error Handling System

1.1 API Error Handler

```php
class RecommendationAPIErrorHandler
{
    protected $retryAttempts = 3;
    protected $retryDelay = 1000; // milliseconds

    public function handle(callable $apiCall, $context = [])
    {
        for ($attempt = 1; $attempt <= $this->retryAttempts; $attempt++) {
            try {
                return $apiCall();
            } catch (APIConnectionException $e) {
                $this->handleConnectionError($e, $attempt);
            } catch (APIRateLimitException $e) {
                $this->handleRateLimitError($e, $attempt);
            } catch (APITimeoutException $e) {
                $this->handleTimeoutError($e, $attempt);
            } catch (\Exception $e) {
                return $this->handleFatalError($e, $context);
            }
        }

        return $this->getFallbackRecommendations($context);
    }

    protected function handleConnectionError($error, $attempt)
    {
        Log::warning("API Connection Error (Attempt {$attempt}): " . $error->getMessage());

        if ($attempt < $this->retryAttempts) {
            $delay = $this->retryDelay * $attempt;
            usleep($delay * 1000); // Convert to microseconds
        }
    }

    protected function handleRateLimitError($error, $attempt)
    {
        $waitTime = $error->getRetryAfter() ?? ($this->retryDelay * 2 * $attempt);
        Log::warning("Rate Limit Hit. Waiting {$waitTime}ms before retry.");

        Cache::put('api_rate_limit_hit', true, now()->addSeconds($waitTime / 1000));
        usleep($waitTime * 1000);
    }
}
```

1.2 Graceful Degradation

```php
class RecommendationDegradation
{
    public function getRecommendations($user_id)
    {
        $strategies = [
            [$this, 'getPrimaryRecommendations'],
            [$this, 'getCachedRecommendations'],
            [$this, 'getSimpleRecommendations'],
            [$this, 'getDefaultRecommendations']
        ];

        foreach ($strategies as $strategy) {
            try {
                $result = $strategy($user_id);
                if ($result->isNotEmpty()) {
                    return $result;
                }
            } catch (\Exception $e) {
                Log::error("Strategy failed: " . get_class($e) . " - " . $e-
>getMessage());
                continue;
            }
        }

        return collect([]); // Empty collection as last resort
    }

    protected function getPrimaryRecommendations($user_id)
    {
        return Cache::remember("primary_recommendations.{$user_id}", now()-
>addMinutes(5), function() use ($user_id) {
            $result = $this->apiHandler->handle(function() use ($user_id) {
                return $this->recommendationService-
>getPersonalizedRecommendations($user_id);
            });

            $this->monitorQuality($result, 'primary');
            return $result;
        });
    }
}
```

2. Fallback Chain Implementation

2.1 Fallback Service

```php
class RecommendationFallbackService
{
    protected $fallbackChain;
    protected $qualityThreshold;

    public function __construct()
    {
```

```php
        $this->fallbackChain = [
            new PersonalizedRecommender(),
            new CategoryBasedRecommender(),
            new PopularityRecommender(),
            new RandomRecommender()
        ];

        $this->qualityThreshold = config('recommendations.quality_threshold', 0.7);
    }

    public function getRecommendations($user_id, array $context = [])
    {
        $results = collect([]);
        $errors = collect([]);

        foreach ($this->fallbackChain as $recommender) {
            try {
                $recommendations = $recommender->getRecommendations($user_id,
$context);

                if ($this->meetsQualityThreshold($recommendations)) {
                    $this->logSuccess($recommender, $recommendations);
                    return $recommendations;
                }

                $results->push([
                    'recommender' => get_class($recommender),
                    'results' => $recommendations
                ]);
            } catch (\Exception $e) {
                $errors->push([
                    'recommender' => get_class($recommender),
                    'error' => $e->getMessage()
                ]);
                continue;
            }
        }

        return $this->getBestAvailableResults($results, $errors);
    }

    protected function meetsQualityThreshold($recommendations)
    {
        return $recommendations->average('confidence_score') >= $this-
>qualityThreshold;
    }
}
```

3. Circuit Breaker Pattern

3.1 API Circuit Breaker

```php
class RecommendationCircuitBreaker
{
    protected $failures = 0;
```

```php
    protected $threshold = 5;
    protected $timeout = 300; // seconds
    protected $lastFailure = null;

    public function execute(callable $operation, callable $fallback)
    {
        if ($this->isOpen()) {
            return $fallback();
        }

        try {
            $result = $operation();
            $this->resetCircuit();
            return $result;
        } catch (\Exception $e) {
            $this->recordFailure();
            return $fallback();
        }
    }

    protected function isOpen()
    {
        if ($this->failures >= $this->threshold) {
            $timeSinceLastFailure = time() - $this->lastFailure;

            if ($timeSinceLastFailure < $this->timeout) {
                return true;
            }

            $this->resetCircuit();
        }

        return false;
    }

    protected function recordFailure()
    {
        $this->failures++;
        $this->lastFailure = time();

        event(new CircuitBreakerTripped([
            'service' => 'recommendations',
            'failures' => $this->failures,
            'timestamp' => $this->lastFailure
        ]));
    }
}
```

4. Monitoring and Recovery

4.1 Health Monitor

```php
class RecommendationHealthMonitor
{
    protected $metrics;
```

```php
    protected $alertThresholds;

    public function trackAPIHealth(string $apiName, callable $operation)
    {
        $startTime = microtime(true);
        $success = false;

        try {
            $result = $operation();
            $success = true;
            return $result;
        } catch (\Exception $e) {
            $this->recordFailure($apiName, $e);
            throw $e;
        } finally {
            $duration = microtime(true) - $startTime;
            $this->recordMetrics($apiName, $duration, $success);
        }
    }

    protected function recordMetrics($apiName, $duration, $success)
    {
        $metrics = [
            'duration' => $duration,
            'success' => $success,
            'timestamp' => now()
        ];

        Redis::hset("api_health:{$apiName}", now()->timestamp,
json_encode($metrics));

        if ($this->shouldAlert($apiName, $metrics)) {
            $this->triggerAlert($apiName, $metrics);
        }
    }

    protected function shouldAlert($apiName, $metrics)
    {
        $recentMetrics = $this->getRecentMetrics($apiName);
        $failureRate = $this->calculateFailureRate($recentMetrics);

        return $failureRate > $this->alertThresholds[$apiName] ?? 0.2;
    }
}
```

4.2 Recovery Strategy

```php
class RecommendationRecoveryManager
{
    public function attemptRecovery($service)
    {
        $recoverySteps = [
            $this->clearCache(),
            $this->resetConnections(),
            $this->refreshTokens(),
```

```php
            $this->restartService()
        ];

        foreach ($recoverySteps as $step) {
            try {
                if ($step()) {
                    $this->verifyServiceHealth();
                    return true;
                }
            } catch (\Exception $e) {
                Log::error("Recovery step failed: " . $e->getMessage());
                continue;
            }
        }

        $this->notifyAdministrators("Service recovery failed for {$service}");
        return false;
    }

    protected function verifyServiceHealth()
    {
        // Implement health checks
        $healthCheck = new HealthCheck();
        $status = $healthCheck->run();

        if (!$status->isHealthy()) {
            throw new RecoveryFailedException($status->getErrors());
        }

        return true;
    }
}
```

Monitoring Services Integration

1. New Relic Integration

1.1 Configuration and Tracking

```php
class NewRelicMonitor
{
    protected $newRelic;

    public function __construct()
    {
        $this->newRelic = new
NewRelicService(config('monitoring.new_relic.license_key'));
    }

    public function monitorRecommendations()
    {
        return new class {
            public function handle($request, Closure $next)
            {
                // Start New Relic transaction
                newrelic_set_appname(config('app.name'));
                newrelic_start_transaction();

                try {
                    // Add custom attributes
                    newrelic_add_custom_parameter('user_id', auth()->id());
                    newrelic_add_custom_parameter('recommendation_type', $request-
>type);

                    $response = $next($request);

                    // Record success metrics
                    newrelic_record_custom_event('Recommendation', [
                        'response_time' => $response->headers->get('X-Response-
Time'),
                        'total_items' => count($response->getData()),
                        'quality_score' => $response->headers->get('X-Quality-Score')
                    ]);

                    return $response;
                } catch (\Exception $e) {
                    // Log error in New Relic
                    newrelic_notice_error($e->getMessage(), $e);
                    throw $e;
                }
            }
        };
    }

    public function recordCustomMetrics($data)
    {
```

```php
        newrelic_custom_metric('Recommendations/responseTime', $data['time']);
        newrelic_custom_metric('Recommendations/precisionScore', $data['precision']);
    }
}
```

1.2 Custom Dashboard

```php
class NewRelicDashboard
{
    public function configureDashboard()
    {
        return [
            'name' => 'Recommendations Dashboard',
            'widgets' => [
                [
                    'title' => 'Recommendations Performance',
                    'visualization' => 'metric_line_chart',
                    'nrql' => "SELECT average(response_time) FROM Recommendation
TIMESERIES"
                ],
                [
                    'title' => 'Success Rate',
                    'visualization' => 'gauge',
                    'nrql' => "SELECT percentage(count(*), WHERE success = true) FROM
Recommendation"
                ]
            ]
        ];
    }
}
```

2. Datadog Integration

2.1 Metrics Tracking

```php
class DatadogMonitor
{
    protected $dogstatsd;

    public function __construct()
    {
        $this->dogstatsd = new DogStatsd([
            'host' => config('monitoring.datadog.host'),
            'port' => config('monitoring.datadog.port')
        ]);
    }

    public function recordMetrics(RecommendationRequest $request, $result)
    {
        // Response time tracking
        $this->dogstatsd->timing('recommendations.response_time', $result['time'], [
            'type' => $request->type,
            'service' => $request->service,
            'environment' => config('app.env')
        ]);
```

```php
        // Recommendations counter
        $this->dogstatsd->increment('recommendations.total', 1, [
            'status' => $result['status'],
            'type' => $request->type
        ]);

        // Quality measurement
        $this->dogstatsd->gauge('recommendations.quality', $result['quality_score'],
[
            'algorithm' => $request->algorithm
        ]);
    }
}
```

3. Elasticsearch Integration

3.1 Advanced Logging

```php
class ElasticSearchLogger
{
    protected $client;

    public function __construct()
    {
        $this->client = ClientBuilder::create()
            ->setHosts([config('monitoring.elasticsearch.host')])
            ->build();
    }

    public function logActivity($data)
    {
        $params = [
            'index' => 'recommendations-' . date('Y.m.d'),
            'body' => [
                'timestamp' => now()->toIso8601String(),
                'user_id' => $data['user_id'],
                'recommendation_type' => $data['type'],
                'recommended_items' => $data['items'],
                'processing_time' => $data['time'],
                'quality_score' => $data['score'],
                'metadata' => [
                    'user_agent' => request()->header('User-Agent'),
                    'ip' => request()->ip(),
                    'session_id' => session()->getId()
                ]
            ]
        ];

        try {
            $response = $this->client->index($params);
            return $response['_id'];
        } catch (\Exception $e) {
            Log::error("Error logging to Elasticsearch: " . $e->getMessage());
            return false;
```

```
        }
    }
}
```

4. Grafana Integration

4.1 Metrics Visualization

```
class GrafanaMetrics
{
    public function configureDashboard()
    {
        return [
            'dashboard' => [
                'title' => 'Recommendation Metrics',
                'panels' => [
                    [
                        'title' => 'System Performance',
                        'type' => 'graph',
                        'targets' => [
                            [
                                'expr' =>
'rate(recommendations_response_time_total[5m])',
                                'legendFormat' => 'Response Time'
                            ]
                        ]
                    ],
                    [
                        'title' => 'Recommendation Quality',
                        'type' => 'heatmap',
                        'targets' => [
                            [
                                'expr' => 'histogram_quantile(0.95,
sum(rate(recommendations_quality_bucket[5m])) by (le))',
                                'legendFormat' => 'Quality Score'
                            ]
                        ]
                    ]
                ]
            ]
        ];
    }
}
```

5. Unified Alert System

5.1 Alert Manager

```
class AlertManager
{
    protected $channels = [
        'slack' => SlackNotifier::class,
        'email' => EmailNotifier::class,
        'sms' => SMSNotifier::class
    ];
```

```php
    protected $levels = [
        'critical' => ['slack', 'email', 'sms'],
        'warning' => ['slack', 'email'],
        'info' => ['slack']
    ];

    public function triggerAlert($level, $message, $context = [])
    {
        foreach ($this->levels[$level] as $channel) {
            $notifier = new $this->channels[$channel];

            try {
                $notifier->send([
                    'message' => $message,
                    'level' => $level,
                    'context' => $context,
                    'timestamp' => now(),
                    'system' => 'Recommendations'
                ]);
            } catch (\Exception $e) {
                Log::error("Error sending alert via {$channel}: " . $e-
>getMessage());
            }
        }
    }
}
```

5.2 Alert Rules

```php
class AlertRules
{
    public function defineRules()
    {
        return [
            'high_latency' => [
                'condition' => 'response_time > 1000',
                'level' => 'warning',
                'message' => 'High latency in recommendation system',
                'time_threshold' => 300, // seconds
                'actions' => [
                    [$this, 'notifyTeam'],
                    [$this, 'scaleResources']
                ]
            ],
            'error_rate' => [
                'condition' => 'error_rate > 0.05',
                'level' => 'critical',
                'message' => 'Error rate above 5%',
                'time_threshold' => 60,
                'actions' => [
                    [$this, 'activateFallback'],
                    [$this, 'notifySRE']
                ]
            ]
```

```
        ];
    }
}
```

www.ingramcontent.com/pod-product-compliance
Lightning Source LLC
La Vergne TN
LVHW092352060326
832902LV00008B/976